Perth
&
Fremantle

Perth city skyline

Fremantle markets

P e r t h

Most visitors find Perth a relaxing city. This is due, in part, to its remoteness from any other major city. Its Mediterranean climate, blessed with many sunny days and mostly fine mild winters, certainly lends itself to the outdoor activities one sees in this picturesque place. People flock to the endless sandy beaches that line Perth's western suburbs or go twilight sailing on the Swan River.

Perth reflects its colonial past, with many old fine buildings still in use today. They add character, set as they are below the huge modern buildings that dominate the skyline.

Western Australia is noted for its spectacular wildflowers, truly one of the wonders of the world when seen in mass in country areas. Even in the city the visitor can, in season, see some stunning displays of wildflowers by visiting Kings Park, one of the finest botanical parks in Australia. The wildflower Festival held every spring is a must for all to see.

On the outskirts of Perth there are many interesting destinations to visit such as Rottnest Island with its unique animal the Quokka, and endless sandy beaches, or the many wineries of the Swan Valley. The hills are not far away, with plenty of National Parks to stroll in. Beyond this are the open fields of the wheatbelt. Here the old colonial character towns of York and Toodyay make a full day's drive a delightful experience.

We hope this small gift book shows you how much Perth and Fremantle have to offer the visitor to this vast State or simply shows others why we live where we live.

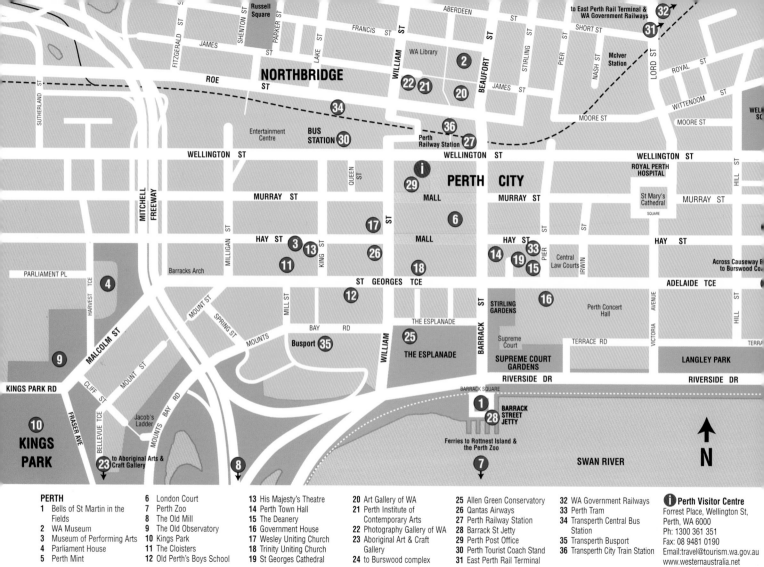

PERTH

1. Bells of St Martin in the Fields
2. WA Museum
3. Museum of Performing Arts
4. Parliament House
5. Perth Mint
6. London Court
7. Perth Zoo
8. The Old Mill
9. The Old Observatory
10. Kings Park
11. The Cloisters
12. Old Perth's Boys School
13. His Majesty's Theatre
14. Perth Town Hall
15. The Deanery
16. Government House
17. Wesley Uniting Church
18. Trinity Uniting Church
19. St Georges Cathedral
20. Art Gallery of WA
21. Perth Institute of Contemporary Arts
22. Photography Gallery of WA
23. Aboriginal Art & Craft Gallery
24. to Burswood complex
25. Allen Green Conservatory
26. Qantas Airways
27. Perth Railway Station
28. Barrack St Jetty
29. Perth Post Office
30. Perth Tourist Coach Stand
31. East Perth Rail Terminal
32. WA Government Railways
33. Perth Tram
34. Transperth Central Bus Station
35. Transperth Busport
36. Transperth City Train Station

ⓘ Perth Visitor Centre
Forrest Place, Wellington St,
Perth, WA 6000
Ph: 1300 361 351
Fax: 08 9481 0190
Email:travel@tourism.wa.gov.au
www.westernaustralia.net

4

Where to go in Perth

One of the most rewarding starts to anyone's first visit to Perth is to drive or walk up to Kings Park. Kings Park is the largest metropolitan park of any Australian capital city with a wealth of wildflowers to view. Whether it is day or night, the views over the city are quite magnificent. You can see the layout of the city which spreads to the edge of the Swan River. Crossing the river below, the Narrows Bridge links the city with the southern suburbs. On the distant horizon is the edge of the Darling Range that runs parallel with the coast for over 200 km.

Just north of the city centre is Northbridge, where many restaurants, hotels and nightclubs offer a wide selection of cuisine and entertainment. For the visitor wishing to purchase gifts, the city centre will give unlimited selections particularly in the Hay Street Mall and around Forrest Place.

Nearby is the Perth Cultural Centre which incorporates the Art Gallery, Western Australian Museum and the State Library. The Art Gallery exhibits wonderful Australian aboriginal paintings and carvings as well as artwork from Australia and overseas while the Museum exhibits Australian cultural and natural history.

Across the river in South Perth is the Perth Zoo. Here one can see a wealth of animals including many species of Australia's unique fauna.

An excellent way to get to know Perth's history is to travel with 'Perth Tram Tours'. They visit most of the main areas of interest.

There are a multitude of other areas to visit particularly in the hills and the Swan Valley. For more in depth information the Western Australian Tourist Centre is a good place to start.

Miriam of the Kinectic Theatre Company

London Court–the arcade was opened in 1937. There are two clocks, one at each end of the arcade that display St George and the Dragon as the clock strikes on the hour.

Hay Street Mall

Forrest place

The Allen Green conservatory

7

Dining out in Perth

There are more restaurants in Perth per head of population than in any other capital city in Australia, so you should have little trouble in finding the cuisine of your choice.

Perth city centre, Subiaco, Mount Lawley, Cottesloe, Claremont, and many other suburbs have a great variety of eating houses. Northbridge, just over the railway line from the Perth city centre, has a very large selection of dining opportunities. For those who wish to enjoy the nightlife of clubs and drinking establishments, Northbridge will also satisfy that need.

The Brass Monkey Hotel - Northbridge

Perth City Buildings
The Old & The New

Nestled between the modern tall buildings are many examples of early colonial architecture. Most have been faithfully restored and are in use to this day.

R & I Bank Building, St Georges Terrace

His Majesty's Theatre, Hay Street

Kings Park

Covering an area of 404 hectares, the park was founded in 1895. The Governor of Western Australia, John Forrest, planted a tree there to commemorate the occasion. Two thirds of the park is natural bushland with 291 species of plants. The remaining third is made up of wonderful cultivated wildflower plants and general recreational areas.

The Botanic Gardens although only 17 ha, contain over 2,000 cultivated native wildflower species. The tall white barked eucalypts that line the drive on Fraser Avenue are Lemon-scented gums, a native tree of the eastern Australia.

Fraser Avenue by day, Kings Park

Fraser Avenue by night, Kings Park

Perth city skyline at sunrise

Perth city skyline at night
Over page–Kangaroo Paws & Wax Flowers in Kings Park

A temporary wildflower exhibit made solely for the annual Wildflower Festival in Kings Park

The Narrows Bridge spanning the Swan River

The ferry jetty at South Perth

The Swan Bells

Within the very modern towering structure are a group (ring) of eighteen bells that are several hundred years old and are one of the few sets of 'Royal Bells.' They were donated to Perth from the famous old church St Martin-in-the-Fields, London to mark Western Australia's Bicentenary. Many people will know the famous nursery rhyme 'Oranges and Lemons' which mentions the 'bells of St Clements' thus reminding us of the bells' antiquity. The bells have been rung since the late fourteenth century.

The Old Windmill, South Perth

The old mill was built in 1835 for William Lockyer and Son. In windy conditions the mill produced twenty five bushels per day. The adjacent miller's cottage contains artifacts of the early pioneer days.

The "Old Windmill", South Perth

The Swan Bells tower

The Old Observatory, West Perth

The observatory was built in 1897 to house the State Astronomer. In the 1960s the Observatory equipment and telescopes were transferred to the new Observatory in Bickley. It is open to visitors by appointment only.

The Burswood Resort Casino

The casino is located on the eastern edge of the city across the Swan River not far from the Causeway Bridge. This extensive five-star complex houses all the sophisticated needs of the visitor including casino, convention centre, sporting facilities including an 18 hole golf course, swimming pools, restaurants and bars.

Rottnest Island

Affectionately called "Rotto" by Western Australians, this would have to be one of the most relaxing places to visit close to Perth. The island lies just eighteen kilometres off the coast and is 11 km long by 4.5 km wide. Its coastline provides wonderful moorings for boats, alternating between rocky cliffs and sandy beaches. The central part of the island has undulating low hills with quite a few salt lakes in the north eastern part of the island. Most of the island is still an 'A' class reserve, protecting the well known marsupial, the Quokka and many plants typical of coastal islands. In geological terms, Rottnest has only been an island for 6,500 years.

The first recorded European to set foot on Rottnest was Samuel Volkerson, commander of the vessel the "Waeckende Boey" in 1658. It was another 38 years before another Dutch vessel DeGeelvinck, commanded by Willem De Vlamingh visited the island. It was he who named the island Rottnest meaning 'Rat's Nest'. When Vlamingh saw the small Quokka, he thought it was a large rat. Not until nearly 200 years later did Captain James Stirling anchor in these waters on his journey to establish the colonial settlement of Swan, named after the unique Australian Black Swan that frequented the Swan Estuary not so long ago.

Perth Beaches

Along the western suburbs of Perth lay a continuous band of sandy beaches on the edge of the vast Indian Ocean. With a climate that Perth enjoys particularly in the summer, people flock in their hundreds to enjoy the cool breezes that flow over the coast. People surf, windsurf, canoe or simply soak up the sun. Do be careful; Australia has one of the highest incidences of skin cancer in the world demonstrating how much sun we really get down under.

For the keen surfer, it stays in your blood for ever–here the guys compare boards

Now there is a new dimension to challenge them–'Kite Surfing'

In Western Australia, more people participate
in fishing than any other recreational sport

Summer hasn't come but still the beaches draw people

Hillarys Boat Harbour

Located in the northern coastal suburb of Sorrento are Sorrento Quay and Hillarys Boat Harbour. This award winning coastal village style complex includes protected beaches, restaurants, cafes, shops and hotel accommodation. The complex is particularly noted for the AQWA. One of the main features of AQWA is a sophisticated underwater tunnel that is completely transparent allowing you to experience the effect of being underwater and close to the variety marine life. Nearby, those who wish to snorkel can explore the limestone reefs. Many of the 136 species of fish which occur where temperate southern waters mingle with tropical waters from the north can be found in this very important marine environment.

Looking across the Swan River to South Perth

Cafes on James Street, Northbridge

Perth Zoo

Located in South Perth, the zoo contains an extensive collection of animal life particularly Australian fauna. Here the big desert Red Kangaroos and Western Grey Kangaroos can be seen at close quarters. Even such rare animals as the Numbat are on view. This small marsupial is Western Australia's animal emblem. There are wetlands, African savanna enclosures, an extensive Australian reptile and bird collection as well as a tropical butterfly house. Keepers and volunteer guides can help you with information.

The Australian Numbat

A peaceful lakeside setting for Australian water fowl in Perth Zoo

Like most international zoos, Perth Zoo houses many exotic animals

Australian Wildlife

Splendid Wren

Red Kangaroo

Black Swans on Lake Monger. Perth.
All the above photographs have been taken in the wild

Pink Cockatoo

Australian Dingo

29

The Mediterranean styled architecture to be seen in the grounds of the University of Western Australia, Crawley

Swan Valley

The region is centred on the upper reaches of the Swan River. Here the alluvial sandy soils have proved an ideal location for growing grapes. A visitor to the Swan Valley can sample the many varieties of wine grown at the various wineries in this locality. Also around the Guildford area are many historical buildings such as Woodbridge House, Guildford Hotel and the Old Guildford Courthouse, Gaol and Museum.

A vineyard near Houghton's winery, Swan Valley

Wine tasting and gift store at Sandalford, Swan Valley

The Hills

Rising from above the Swan Coastal Plain in the eastern suburbs of Perth is the Darling Range, affectionately known as 'the Hills'. The surface soils consist predominantly of laterite. From this soil bauxite is derived which is used in the production of aluminium. Under these surface soils lie some of the oldest granite rocks in the world.

The Hills are not far from the city and here you can visit orchards, craft stores or simply find peace and quiet in one of the many National Parks that are located in the range.

Mount Dale   John Forrest Falls–John Forrest Natio

Gooseberry Hill in spring time

Acacias in full bloom in the Wandoo woodland, Avon Valley National Park

Noble Spider Orchid *Caladenia varians subsp. noblis*

Springtime on the Darling scarp

Fuchsia Grevillea *Grevillea bipinnatifida*

Fremantle

Fremantle has a character all of its own. The fine old buildings have been faithfully restored and the markets, cappuccino strip and harbour restaurants offer the visitor a relaxed, inviting atmosphere. There are many reminders of the early colonial days such as the Fremantle Prison, the Round House, the Maritime Museum and the Fremantle Arts Centre. Set on the mouth of the Swan River, Fremantle is still the major working port for Western Australia moving many millions of tonnes of cargo a year, and the bustle of the harbour sits comfortably with the historic atmosphere and fine buildings. For many visitors, Fremantle is one of the major highlights of their stay in this large State, with so much to see and do.

Street artists enthrall onlookers outside the Sail and Anchor Hotel

Fremantle

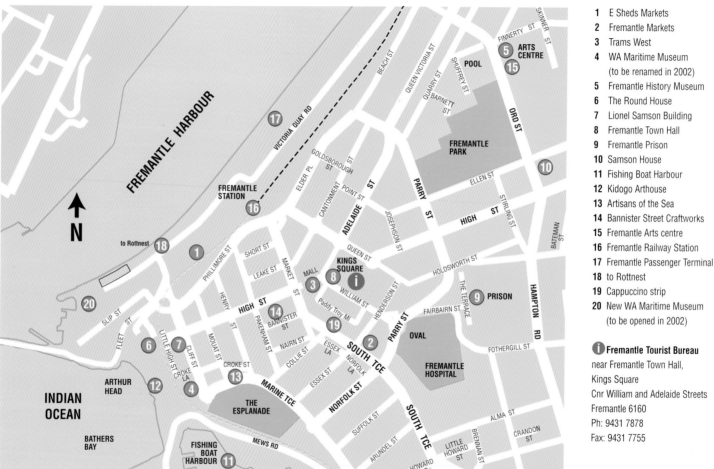

1 E Sheds Markets
2 Fremantle Markets
3 Trams West
4 WA Maritime Museum
   (to be renamed in 2002)
5 Fremantle History Museum
6 The Round House
7 Lionel Samson Building
8 Fremantle Town Hall
9 Fremantle Prison
10 Samson House
11 Fishing Boat Harbour
12 Kidogo Arthouse
13 Artisans of the Sea
14 Bannister Street Craftworks
15 Fremantle Arts centre
16 Fremantle Railway Station
17 Fremantle Passenger Terminal
18 to Rottnest
19 Cappuccino strip
20 New WA Maritime Museum
   (to be opened in 2002)

ⓘ Fremantle Tourist Bureau
near Fremantle Town Hall,
Kings Square
Cnr William and Adelaide Streets
Fremantle 6160
Ph: 9431 7878
Fax: 9431 7755

Map copyright City of Fremantle 2001

Where to go in Fremantle

Having arrived in Fremantle, why not take a quick break and sit on the 'Cappuccino Strip' and let Fremantle's relaxed lifestyle slow you down. You can then get orientated to this historical old port town.

One of the best ways to familiarise yourself with Fremantle and it's history is to take one the 'Trams West' guided tram tours. This is an excellent way to get to know the many locations and the history behind them. On foot, you can walk across the Esplanade Park to the harbour with its many restaurants and cafes on the harbourside. Opposite the northern side of the park is the Western Australian Maritime Museum which is open 10.30-5 p.m. daily. There are excellent maritime exhibits housed in the old building. In 2002 there will be a very modern maritime museum located on the Fremantle Wharf near Victoria Quay.

Most of the popular historical sites are illustrated in this book and located on the map opposite.

A visit to the Fremantle Prison will give the visitor an opportunity to see and feel what it was like to be a prisoner not only in the early colonial days but also in very recent times. The prison was closed in 1993.

At the western end of High Street is one of the first buildings erected, the Round House. Here you will get excellent views of the city and the fishing boat harbour.

Although it is a reasonable walk to the Fremantle Arts Museum, the visitor will find this one of the best exhibits of early colonial artifacts and also excellent modern art and crafts. The grounds are set behind high stone walls and make a peaceful retreat . You can also have meals at the cafe located inside.

Just a short walk away from the Fremantle Arts Centre is Sampson House on the corner of Ord and Ellen Streets. Sadly, few people get to see this little gem of a house containing artifacts and furniture typical of an early colonial dwelling–open 1-5 p.m. Sundays.

For more in depth information, you can visit the Fremantle Tourist Bureau located near the Town Hall on Kings Square. They can help you with any information you may require and can make bookings for tours or accommodation. You can also contact them by phoning 08 94317878.

"Ravi" gets the visitors to Fremantle involved in her difficult balancing routine

A street artist holds a captivated audience on the cappuccino strip

Juggling fire sticks up a six metre pole is no easy task

The Cappuccino Strip

Here in Fremantle not only tourists but many locals flock to relax in the casual atmosphere. There are countless restaurants, coffee houses and hotels from which to choose.

Gino's—one of the first of the early establishments along the strip

The well known Sail and Anchor Hotel

Overpage, Fremantle's cappuccino strip

Fremantle Markets

The markets have been in operation for over 100 years. The foundation stone for the site of the Fremantle Markets was laid by the State's first Premier, Sir John Forrest, in 1897.

They are a popular attraction both for international visitors and for the people of Perth selling not only fresh produce but also a wide range of clothing, homeware and gifts.

The opening hours are 9 a.m.-9 p.m. Friday, 9 a.m.-5 p.m. Saturday, 10 a.m.-5 p.m. Sunday and on public holiday Mondays only, from 9 a.m.-5 p.m.

The Fremantle Markets

Fruit and vegetables in the Fremantle Markets

Fremantle Prison

Construction of the prison commenced in 1851 with the main buildings being completed in 1859. It is ironic that those who built the prison were convicts themselves. They were brought out from the British Isles and housed in the prison from 1855 .

Convicts were brought to Fremantle between the years 1850 and 1868.
The prison was not decommissioned until 1993, having been in service for one hundred and thirty six years. It is open between 10 a.m.-6.00 p.m. daily.

Western Australian Maritime Museum

One of the many buildings in Fremantle constructed by early convict labour
in the 1850s, the museum now houses maritime artifacts from the many
shipwrecks that have been found along the Western Australian coast.

Fremantle Town Hall

Built in 1887, the Town Hall was the seat of the Fremantle Council until
the mid 1960s. The inauguration was marred by a tragic event. The
licensee of the National Hotel, William Conroy tried to attend the evening
functions in a drunken state. The city councillor, a Mr Snook ,duly denied
him entry. Conroy subsequently returned and shot councillor Snook who
later died. Conroy was hanged in November of that year.

Fremantle History Museum and Arts Centre

The Fremantle Arts Centre building has had an interesting history. For most of its life it was in use as a so called 'lunatic asylum' or 'prison hospital for psychiatric patients'. It was then a training hospital for midwives and then a base for US naval personnel. Before being restored and used as a museum and arts centre. Within the museum are many exhibits of early colonial artifacts and history. The Arts Centre has a few galleries exhibiting modern day arts and crafts. As you can see from above, artists and sculptors enjoy the pleasant, peaceful environment of the Arts Centre grounds.

The museum is open Thursday-Sunday 1.00-5.00 p.m. and the Arts Centre 10.00 a.m.-5.00 p.m. daily and Wednesday 7.00-9.00 p.m..

The Old & The New

The early colonial architecture of Fremantle represents one of the most extensive examples of this type of port city. Here the majority of buildings retain their original appearance having been faithfully restored and are in use to this day. It is a town where modern buildings have to take a back seat, a pleasant change from many modern cities.

ARTISANS ⁰F THE SEA

"Artisans of the Sea", a subsidiary company of the M.G. Kailis Group (a pearling company). This fine building was originally a Savings Bank built in 1903. It has now been faithfully restored and is in use to this day.

The Round House

Henry Street

The New

To cater for the varied requirements of the many visitors to Fremantle, the city provides an extensive range of modern facilities including cinemas, numerous restaurants and nightclubs.

Over the previous pages you have seen much of the creations of 'mankind' in a city environment. If you travel this vast, wonderful state, you will see creations of a grander scale by a 'greater force', whose land the Australian Aborigines have danced and sung on for thousands of years—go see and enjoy.

Simon Nevill

Simon has taken on many occupations through his life. Being a qualified furniture designer he spent much of his life in the interior and furniture design world but his real love and passion has been the study of natural history and the protection of the environment. Having led birdwatching tours worldwide for over fourteen years now, Simon is concentrating on producing books to bring his love of the outdoors to all.

Dedication

During the production of the book, the United States of America experienced a terrible tragedy on the 11th September, 2001. This book is dedicated not only to all the innocent people who lost their lives on that fateful day, but to all the innocent people of the world who have perished through man's inhumanity to man. It is hoped that all the various religions of the world can develop tolerance of peoples differing beliefs and also, that no country should try to dominate another, through expansionist means based on greed and power.